D1377214

EDGE
BOOKS

THIS or THAT

HISTORY

Debate

A RIP-ROARING GAME OF EITHER/OR QUESTIONS

BY Michael O'HEARN

CAPSTONE PRESS
a capstone imprint

Edge Books are published by Capstone Press,
1710 Roe Crest Drive, North Mankato, Minnesota 56003.
www.capstonepub.com

Library of Congress Cataloging-in-Publication Data
O'Hearn, Michael, 1972–
   This or that history debate : a rip-roaring game of either/or questions / by
      Michael O'Hearn.
      p. cm. — (Edge books : this or that?)
   Includes bibliographical references.
   Summary: "Offers intriguing either/or questions and content on history topics to
      encourage critical thinking and debate"—Provided by publisher.
   ISBN 978-1-4296-8414-9 (library binding)
   ISBN 978-1-4296-9274-8 (paperback)
   ISBN 978-1-62065-235-0 (ebook PDF)
   1. History—Juvenile literature. I. Title.
   D10.O36 2013
   909—dc23   2012002218

Editorial Credits
Kristen Mohn, editor; Veronica Correia, designer; Eric Gohl, media researcher;
   Laura Manthe, production specialist

Photo Credits
Alamy: North Wind Picture Archives, 6; Corbis: Bettmann, 21; Dreamstime: Darryl
Brooks, 23; iStockphoto: Duncan Walker, 10, 11; Library of Congress: 14, 20, 26, 28,
Chronicling America/University of California, Riverside; Riverside, CA, 8; Newscom:
Peter Connolly/akg-images, 25, WHA/United Archives/KPA, 18; Shutterstock: Antonio
Abrignani, 13, Balu, 3, funhare, cover (top left), James Horning, 5, Makhnach, cover
(bottom right), Matt Ragen, 4, optimarc, cover & interior (background), Paul Cowan,
22 (all), Petrafler, 1, 15; Wikimedia: Public Domain, 7, 9, 12, 16, 17, 19, 24, 27, 29

Printed in the United States of America in Stevens Point, Wisconsin.
032012   006678WZF12

HOW TO USE THIS BOOK:

Ever wondered what it would be like to be part of history? Would you have the bravery to be a medieval knight or a samurai warrior? Would you rather take your chances on the *Titanic* or the *Hindenburg*? What if you had to pick one or the other?

This book is full of questions that take you inside the marvels and mysteries of history. The questions are followed by information to help you weigh the options and make a choice. But don't worry—it's not a test! There are no wrong answers.

When you are finished reading the book, try it out with your family and friends. Decide how you would make history ... if you had a choice!

THIS

ALCATRAZ

- designed to be escape-proof
- harsh discipline such as wearing a ball and chain
- 5 x 9-foot (1.5 x 2.7-meter) cells

Opened in 1934, Alcatraz was a federal prison built on a small island in San Francisco Bay. It held the worst criminals of the day—mobsters and murderers. Alcatraz prisoners lived in small, windowless cells. They marched silently to breakfast, lunch, and dinner, unless they misbehaved. Then they were put in a dark cell called "the hole" and given only bread and water. Lucky inmates earned work assignments, such as making clothes for the military. Over the years, 36 men tried to escape. Most were caught. Eight were killed. The fate of five is unknown. Did they drown or make it to freedom?

OR THAT?

TO BE A PRISONER IN
A MEDIEVAL DUNGEON

- pitch dark
- cold and damp
- no toilet

During medieval times (about AD 400–1500) there were no prisons. But that doesn't mean there was no punishment. Common thieves and religious lawbreakers were sometimes held in dungeons deep beneath castles. There, they might be tortured to confess their crimes or left to die. Others were hanged or burned at the stake. Those who made it out alive might have a mark burned into their skin or have a hand cut off.

THIS

THE LOST ROANOKE COLONY

- few artifacts or clues
- water may now cover the original colony site because of rising ocean levels
- 425-year-old mystery

In 1587 a group of 117 men, women, and children landed on Roanoke Island. It was located off what is now the North Carolina coast. They planned to build England's first settlement in America. Three years later, the supply ship returned, but the colonists had disappeared. The word "Croatoan" was carved on a tree. Croatoan was the name of a local tribe. Did the colonists move or perish? Today the exact location of the colony and the fate of the colonists are unknown.

OR THAT?

AMELIA EARHART'S DISAPPEARANCE

- lost while searching for 0.7-square-mile (1.8-square-kilometer) island
- unknown whether crash was in ocean or on an island
- search ships found no wreckage

Amelia Earhart was the first woman to fly across the Atlantic Ocean solo. In 1937 she tried to become the first woman to fly all 29,000 miles (46,700 km) around the world. Earhart and her navigator, Fred Noonan, planned to end the flight in California. Earhart was scheduled to make a refueling stop on tiny Howland Island in the Pacific Ocean. She never reached the island. But her radio messages to a waiting ship showed that she flew incredibly close. Still, neither the crew nor Earhart could determine her exact location. Eventually, her messages stopped. Earhart, Noonan, and their plane were never found.

THIS

TO HAVE SAiLED ON THE TITANIC

- luxury ship nearly three football fields in length
- only enough lifeboats for about half on board
- passengers endured 2½ hours of panic as the ship slowly sank

In 1912 the *Titanic* sailed from England for New York City on its first official voyage. Passengers enjoyed four days of smooth sailing. The largest passenger ship at the time, *Titanic* carried about 2,200 people. But the final report stated that only 705 survived the trip. Despite seven iceberg warnings from nearby ships, *Titanic* crashed into an iceberg the night of April 14th. Within three hours, the ship sank into the icy Atlantic Ocean. The lifeboats had seats for 1,178 people, but only about 700 of those seats were filled. Most other passengers went down with the ship or died in the cold water while waiting for rescue.

OR *THAT*?

TO HAVE FLOWN ON THE
HINDENBURG

- traveled 80 miles (129 km) per hour—faster than ships
- dangerously high winds at landing site
- fire consumed the ship in just 37 seconds

For a year the massive airship Hindenburg carried wealthy passengers across the Atlantic Ocean between Germany and the United States. The 800-foot- (244-m-) long blimp provided comfortable living space and fantastic views of the sky. But on May 6, 1937, something went terribly wrong near the landing site in New Jersey. The hydrogen gas that made the blimp lighter than air was highly flammable. As the Hindenburg tried to land, the gas ignited and the ship was swallowed by flames. The mighty Hindenburg fell to the ground. Of the 97 on board, 35 were killed.

THIS

CALIFORNIA GOLD RUSH

- few miners struck it rich
- overpriced supplies
- malnutrition and disease such as land scurvy were common

Rivers flowing down from the Sierra Nevada Mountains carried gold dust and nuggets. Lucky miners collected them during California's Gold Rush. Beginning in 1849, miners from across the country and around the world flooded the area. They hoped to strike it rich. But most of these people, known as forty-niners, discovered only backbreaking work. They spent hours digging, sifting, and moving rocks. The miners found barely enough gold to cover the steep prices of supplies sold by greedy merchants. Worst of all, dirty living conditions and diets without fruits and vegetables led to diseases and often death.

OR THAT?

- booty often split among the shipmates
- cruel captains
- deadly combat

TO SEEK FORTUNE ABOARD A

PIRATE SHIP

In the early 1700s, pirate flags like the skull and crossbones brought fear to ships throughout the Atlantic Ocean. Pirate captains like Blackbeard and Black Bart led their lawless bands on raids of merchant ships. They stole cargo including silver, gold, silk, sugar, and other goods. The pirate life was a dangerous one. It was filled with ship-to-ship cannon battles and hand-to-hand combat. Naval warships hunted pirate ships. If found guilty of piracy in court, the captured pirates were sometimes hanged.

THIS

INUIT LIVING IN AN IGLOO

- deadly cold
- long periods of darkness
- challenging hunts

Northern Canada, Alaska, and Greenland are home to the Inuit people. In these Arctic regions, temperatures sometimes drop to minus 50 degrees Fahrenheit (minus 46 degrees Celsius) or colder. Until the mid-1900s, many Inuit lived in huts made of whalebone or wood. In the winter they covered huts with blocks of snow to protect against the cold. These huts were called igloos. On hunting trips they would build temporary igloos made entirely of snow blocks. The Inuit hunted whales, seals, polar bears, and caribou. They ate most meat raw.

OR **THAT?**

TO BE AN 1800s PLAINS INDIAN LIVING IN A TEPEE

- extreme conditions—high wind speeds, thunderstorms, blizzards, or hot temperatures
- relied on buffalo for food, shelter, clothing, and tools
- white settlers took land and killed buffalo

Most American Indian tribes on the Great Plains of the United States lived in tepees. These surprisingly sturdy dwellings were made of several long poles covered with buffalo hides. A campfire could be lit inside the tepee and smoke would escape out a hole at the top. Most importantly, tepees could be taken apart and moved. Tribes moved often to follow buffalo herds or to escape enemy attacks. White settlers sometimes pushed tribes from their land. Women were responsible for the quick building and moving of the tepees. Two women could build a tepee in about an hour.

THIS

TO BE A
SAMURAI
WARRIOR

- constant warring
- equally skilled samurai opponents
- unquestioning obedience to leaders

The Japanese samurai were dedicated to the study of hand-to-hand and weapons combat. They included among their ranks archers, spearmen, and cavalrymen. All of these warriors wielded the long, curved katana, or samurai sword. Until the mid-1800s, Japanese clans battled one another with the samurai as their soldiers. Samurai warriors were proud and committed to their clan. They feared death so little that they would rather die than be captured by an enemy.

OR THAT?

TO BE A
MEDIEVAL KNIGHT

- heavy armor
- often fought on horseback
- long stretches at war

Mounted on an armored warhorse, a knight rode into battle carrying a lance or sword. These European warriors began their horse and weapons training at an early age. Jousting tournaments served to sharpen their battle skills. Knights served a lord or king and lived by a code of chivalry. This code required brave and noble behavior. Knights often waged wars in distant lands that lasted many years.

THIS

TO HAVE HELPED BUILD
MOUNT RUSHMORE

- frightening heights
- physically demanding work
- took 14 years to complete

Carved into a granite mountainside in the Black Hills of South Dakota is a monument to American presidents. It features the faces of George Washington, Thomas Jefferson, Abraham Lincoln, and Theodore Roosevelt. Building began in 1927. More than 400 workers used dynamite, jackhammers, drills, and chisels to clear away 450,000 tons (408,000 metric tons) of rock. The men worked while strapped in harnesses or standing on platforms. They dangled by cables from the 5,725-foot (1,745-m) mountaintop. Even with these dangerous conditions, no deaths occurred during the building of the monument.

or THAT?

TO HAVE HELPED BUILD THE PANAMA CANAL

- worldwide importance
- deadly diseases spread quickly
- 120°F (49°C) temperatures

In August 1914 the Panama Canal opened. It was a man-made waterway for shipping between the Atlantic and Pacific Oceans. The canal took more than 50,000 workers 10 years to complete. Giant steam shovels moved 8-ton (7.3-metric ton) buckets of earth to trains that carried it away. Workers drilled holes in massive rocks and blasted them with dynamite. They faced dangers from explosions as well as diseases such as malaria and yellow fever. Mudslides were another threat. More than 5,000 men died during the U.S. effort to build the canal.

THIS

THE IRISH POTATO FAMINE

- main food source destroyed
- sickness was widespread
- many lived in poverty even before famine

When a disease called blight struck Ireland's potato crop in 1845, the results were deadly. At the time of the famine, the English owned most of the land. The Irish were left with small plots to farm for themselves. They relied on the most abundant crop for food—potatoes. When blight infected the potatoes, the country had no other crop to harvest. People had little money to buy other food. Poor diet and unclean conditions led to diseases such as dysentery and typhus. One million people died. Two million others left Ireland for the United States or other countries.

OR THAT?

TO HAVE LIVED THROUGH THE GREAT DEPRESSION

- few jobs available
- widespread homelessness
- relied on handouts to survive

In 1929 the U.S. stock market crashed. People lost large amounts of money. Soon after, many banks closed. This was the start of the Great Depression and it lasted for more than 10 years. Twenty-five percent of U.S. workers were unemployed. Hundreds of people would mob a business at the rumor of one job. Jobless adults and teenagers traveled on freight trains looking for work. Many families couldn't afford rent or house payments. They moved into shelters made of scrap wood and cardboard. Hungry people stood in long lines for free soup and bread.

THIS

BABE RUTH "CALL HIS SHOT"

- game 3 of 1932 World Series
- tied 4 to 4 in 5th inning
- 51,000 Chicago Cubs fans attended

George Herman "Babe" Ruth hit a home run about every 12 at-bats. And none is more famed—or disputed—than "The Called Shot." Ruth was at bat with two strikes in the count. He held his arm out toward center field with two fingers extended. Some, including Ruth, say he was pointing to where his ball would go. Others say he was counting strikes. Either way, he launched a deep drive over the center field wall. A grainy film captured the moment but never settled the dispute.

OR THAT?

TO HAVE SEEN SECRETARIAT WIN THE TRIPLE CROWN

- three races in five weeks
- Secretariat set track or world records at all three races
- competed against a total of 21 other horses

The Triple Crown is a true test of a racehorse's talent. To earn the Crown, a horse must win the Kentucky Derby, the Preakness Stakes, and the Belmont Stakes. Since 1919, 21 horses have won the first two races. Only 11 have won all three. And none of them performed like Secretariat did in 1973. He won the Derby in record time and the Preakness by 2 ½ horse lengths. Then, three weeks later, Secretariat won the Belmont by an amazing 31 horse lengths.

THIS

TO EAT HAGGIS

- high in protein, but also high in salt and fat
- ancient Greeks may have been the first to eat haggis
- mixture stuffed in a casing like sausage

For hundreds of years, the Scottish ate every edible part of the sheep, including the liver, lungs, and heart. These organs would spoil quickly so they were eaten first in a dish called haggis. The cook would chop the organs and add sheep fat, oatmeal, and spices. Then the mix was boiled inside the sheep's stomach. Many people still eat haggis today.

OR THAT?

TO HUNT AND EAT
WOOLLY MAMMOTH

- dangerous prey
- animals were cornered in ravines or watering holes
- butchering was done at the kill site

The woolly mammoth had long, deadly tusks. It weighed up to 8 tons (7.3 metric tons) and stood about 12 feet (3.7 m) high. Its size made it a hard animal to kill with early weapons. But 11,000 years ago, hunters in North America took down the dangerous beasts with stone-tipped spears. They might follow a mammoth for days. They kept throwing spears at it and waited for the animal to weaken from its injuries. After the kill, the meat was dried and stored. It would feed the hunters' families for months.

THIS

- 9,000 Allied soldiers killed or wounded
- sea-to-land assault
- gray skies and choppy seas

American and British Allied troops invaded Normandy, France, on June 6, 1944. It was the turning point of World War II (1939–1945). At the time, Germany occupied much of Europe, including northern France. About 160,000 Allied troops stormed a 50-mile (80-km) stretch of French beaches on D-Day. The soldiers were transported to the beaches by more than 800 ships. Then they plowed through rough surf, mines, and enemy machine-gun fire toward the powerful Germans. The Allies took the beach, and by August, the capital city of Paris was free.

OR THAT?

TO HAVE FOUGHT WITH THE SPARTANS AT THE BATTLE OF THERMOPYLAE

- Spartans were heavily outnumbered
- Spartans fought to the last man
- boys from Sparta were taken from home at age 7 to train as warriors

In 480 BC a Persian army of about 300,000 soldiers invaded Greece. The Greek city-state of Sparta had only 300 soldiers. But they led 11,000 other Greeks in the fight against Persia at a narrow beach at Thermopylae. The beach faced a mountainside. It was only 50 feet (15 m) wide in some places. This small space helped limit the number of invaders the Spartans had to fight at one time. Every last Spartan was killed in the fight. But they managed to hold back the Persian army. This allowed their fellow Greek soldiers to escape.

THIS

TO BE AN
OLD WEST OUTLAW

- lynchings, shoot-outs, and hangings
- "Dead or alive" rewards offered for outlaws
- armed townspeople often hunted outlaws

infamous Old West outlaw Jesse James

The late 1800s and early 1900s in the western United States is the period known as the Old West. During this time some men chose the outlaw life. Stealing horses or robbing banks, trains, or stagecoaches could all lead to quick fortune. But living outside the law also meant a life of hiding. Outlaws were always running from sheriffs and bounty hunters. Posters encouraged citizens to hunt down outlaws and bring them to the police—dead or alive. The life of an outlaw often ended with a bullet or by hanging from a noose.

OR THAT?

TO BE A ROARING '20s GANGSTER

- deadly competition between gangs
- gangsters often were captured or killed by FBI agents
- used dangerous submachine guns called Tommy guns

infamous 1920s gangster Al Capone

Organized crime grew quickly and violently in the 1920s when the United States outlawed alcohol. Gangsters stepped in to meet the demand, making and selling illegal alcohol. The gangs who ran these activities fought bloody wars for a larger share of the business. They also robbed banks and led illegal gambling operations. Gangsters often made a lot of money and lived in fancy mansions. But they were also constantly chased by local police and FBI agents. Many gangsters were killed by enemy gangs. Others ended up trading their mansions for jail cells when the law caught up with them.

THIS

ANCIENT EGYPTIAN DESERT CARAVAN

- lack of water
- often traveled at night to avoid the blistering sun
- burned camel dung for fires

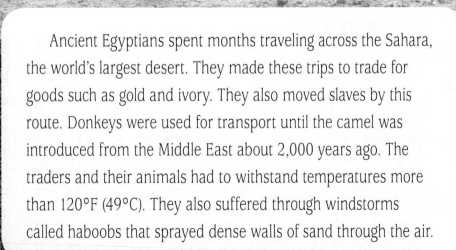

Ancient Egyptians spent months traveling across the Sahara, the world's largest desert. They made these trips to trade for goods such as gold and ivory. They also moved slaves by this route. Donkeys were used for transport until the camel was introduced from the Middle East about 2,000 years ago. The traders and their animals had to withstand temperatures more than 120°F (49°C). They also suffered through windstorms called haboobs that sprayed dense walls of sand through the air.

OR THAT?

TO TRAVEL IN AN AMERICAN WAGON TRAIN

- rough terrain and steep mountain passes
- run-ins with American Indian tribes
- broken equipment hard to fix

In the 1840s settlers began moving west to California and Oregon. They hoped to find land to farm. The Oregon Trail started in Missouri and crossed mountains, deserts, rivers, and forests. Settlers traveled in groups of covered wagons pulled by oxen. Some wagons carried more than 2 tons (1.8 metric tons) of supplies. The settlers might travel 10 to 15 miles (16 to 24 km) a day for four to six months. They traded with American Indians along the way, but sometimes also fought against them. Other struggles included broken wagon wheels. These took a long time to fix and often required tools they didn't have.

LIGHTNING ROUND:

☆ Would you choose to have invented the TELEPHONE or the TOILET?

☆ Would you choose to ride an ELEPHANT INTO ANCIENT BATTLE or a TANK INTO MODERN WAR?

☆ Would you choose to have CREATED A FAMOUS COMIC BOOK SUPERHERO or have CURED A DEADLY DISEASE?

☆ Would you choose to be an 1800s WHALING SHIP CAPTAIN or a BIG GAME HUNTER IN AFRICA?

☆ Would you choose to hear MOZART IN CONCERT or watch PICASSO PAINT?

☆ Would you choose to cross the DELAWARE RIVER WITH GEORGE WASHINGTON DURING THE AMERICAN REVOLUTION or defend the ALAMO WITH JIM BOWIE IN THE TEXAS WAR OF INDEPENDENCE?

☆ Would you choose to search for the FOUNTAIN OF YOUTH or EL DORADO, THE LOST CITY OF GOLD?

☆ Would you choose to be a VIKING WARRIOR or a MONGOL WARRIOR?

☆ Would you choose to ride for the PONY EXPRESS or explore with LOUIS AND CLARK?

☆ Would you choose to be a PHARAOH IN ANCIENT EGYPT or a KING IN MEDIEVAL EUROPE?

☆ Would you choose to drive a FORD MODEL T or a ROMAN CHARIOT?

☆ Would you choose to build the GREAT WALL OF CHINA or an EGYPTIAN PYRAMID?

☆ Would you choose to attend a ONE-ROOM SCHOOLHOUSE IN THE 1800s or skip school to WORK ON THE FARM?

☆ Would you choose to work in a FACTORY IN THE INDUSTRIAL REVOLUTION or as a serf during THE MIDDLE AGES?

☆ Would you choose to travel to Antarctica with THE SHACKLETON EXPEDITION or sail to America with CHRISTOPHER COLUMBUS?

☆ Would you choose to live without MODERN PLUMBING or MODERN ELECTRICITY?

☆ Would you choose to BE TRIED AS A WITCH AT SALEM or BE BLACKLISTED DURING THE RED SCARE?

☆ Would you choose to fight in THE CIVIL WAR or in WORLD WAR II?

☆ Would you choose to be a ROMAN SOLDIER or a JAPANESE NINJA?

☆ Would you choose to meet BENJAMIN FRANKLIN or THOMAS EDISON?

☆ Would you choose to fly an airplane with THE WRIGHT BROTHERS or fly to the moon with NEIL ARMSTRONG?

READ MORE

Dougherty, Terri. *300 Heroes: The Battle of Thermopylae.* Bloodiest Battles. Mankato, Minn.: Capstone Press, 2009.

Hanel, Rachael. *Life as a Knight: An Interactive History Adventure.* You Choose Books. Warriors. Mankato, Minn.: Capstone Press, 2010.

Morley, Jacqueline. *You Wouldn't Want to Live in a Medieval Castle!: A Home You'd Rather Not Inhabit.* New York: Franklin Watts, 2009.

INTERNET SITES

FactHound offers a safe, fun way to find Internet sites related to this book. All of the sites on FactHound have been researched by our staff.

Here's all you do:

Visit *www.facthound.com*

Type in this code: 9781429684149

Check out projects, games and lots more at
www.capstonekids.com